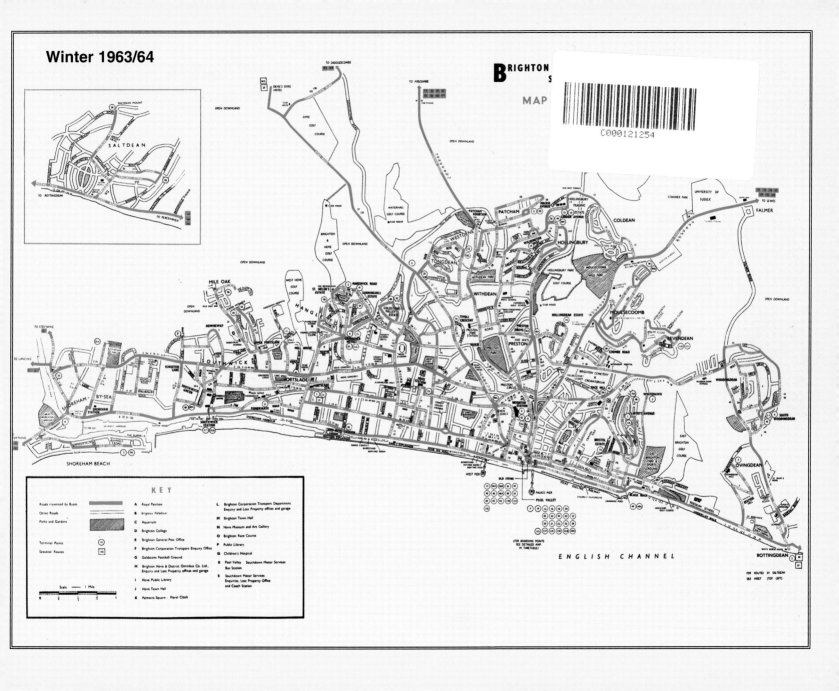

Winter 1963/64

BRIGHTON
S
MAP

SALTDEAN

TO ROTTINGDEAN

TO PEACEHAVEN

ENGLISH CHANNEL

ROTTINGDEAN

FOR ROUTES IN SALTDEAN
SEE INSET (TOP LEFT)

KEY

Roads traversed by Buses

Other Roads

Parks and Gardens

Terminal Points

Seasonal Routes

Scale — 1 Mile

A — Royal Pavilion
B — Brighton Palladium
C — Aquarium
D — Brighton College
E — Brighton General Post Office
F — Brighton Corporation Transport Enquiry Office
G — Goldstone Football Ground
H — Brighton Hove & District Omnibus Co. Ltd., Enquiry and Lost Property offices and garage
I — Hove Public Library
J — Hove Town Hall
K — Palmeira Square : Floral Clock

L — Brighton Corporation Transport Department Enquiry and Lost Property offices and garage
M — Brighton Town Hall
N — Hove Museum and Art Gallery
O — Brighton Race Course
P — Public Library
Q — Children's Hospital
R — Pool Valley Southdown Motor Services Bus Station
S — Southdown Motor Services Enquiries, Lost Property Office and Coach Station

(FOR BOARDING POINTS
SEE DETAILED MAP
IN TIMETABLE)

Streets of Brighton

**Glyn Kraemer-Johnson
& John Bishop**

Introduction

Elegant Regency crescents and terraces, hot-dog and whelk stalls, mean back streets, the Lanes with their quaint antique shops, sprawling estates, busy shopping thoroughfares, tree-lined avenues and beautifully kept parks and gardens.

It has been called 'the Queen of Watering Places', 'London by the sea' and 'Doctor Brighton'. It is famous for its Royal Pavilion — summer palace of the Prince Regent (later George IV) — and for its two Victorian piers, although one is now in a sad state of disrepair.

Visitors were attracted initially by the curing properties of the sea, and in Edwardian times it became one of the 'places to be' when fashionable young ladies would promenade along the seafront in the hope of catching the eye of a suitable beau. The coming of the railway and, in particular, its electrification in the 1930s brought the town within easy reach of London, and on summer weekends day-trippers in their thousands would pour out of the station and down Queen's Road to the seafront.

The boom continued after World War 2 and until the early 'Sixties, when the opening of Sussex University at Falmer on the outskirts of the town coincided with the rise in popularity of holidays abroad. Equal to the challenge, Brighton underwent another reincarnation. Many of its numerous cinemas and theatres closed, to be replaced by nightclubs, discos and casinos. It took on a younger, more vibrant atmosphere, brought about by the many students, both local and from overseas, who throng the town all year round. Now it has its pavement cafés, its buskers and street entertainers, its trendy shops. Many of its fine Regency houses have been converted into flats, while others still house the famous — actors, playwrights and artists. It still has its detached houses in quiet suburbs as well as its large estates, and the rows of two-up, two-down Victorian houses, of which there are many, are now advertised as 'bijou town cottages'.

These, then, are the streets of Brighton, offering contrasts that span the whole social spectrum. And the transport scene is just as varied.

For many years Brighton was served by three operators — a Tilling company, a BET subsidiary and a municipality. Brighton Corporation operated a fleet of open-top trams from its formation in 1901 until 1939, when it replaced them with a fleet of AEC trolley- and motor buses. Together with some postwar BUTs, the trolleybuses lasted until 1961, when they were replaced by Leyland PD2s. An agreement reached in 1938 between the Corporation and Brighton, Hove & District (the Tilling Group operator) meant that livery, fleetnames and destination displays were common between the two operators.

Brighton, Hove & District (BH&D) was formed in 1935 from the Brighton operations of Thomas Tilling. The original BH&D fleet consisted mainly of Tilling STs and STLs — AEC Regents with bodies by Tilling or Dodson, many of which were built at the former Tilling premises in Holland Road, Hove. The Bristol made its appearance in 1936, and, as with other Tilling-group

---

Front cover: In the late 1950s one could visit Brighton and in the hub of Brighton Corporation's empire at the Old Steine one could quite effortlessly take this view. This really shows how the scene was inherited from the tram era when this was also the hub of the tram routes. No 92 (KCD 92), an AEC Regent III with Weymann bodywork, deputises for a trolleybus on route 46A whilst trolleybus 6 stands behind and 20 awaits duty on the 46. The Corporation Inspector stands looking at the nearside screen as if in disbelief that a motor bus has sneaked onto a trolleybus route! *Marcus Eavis*

Previous page: Patcham, in north Brighton, was served by BH&D's 5 group of routes as well as Southdown's 15. The terminus of the 5 was (and is) the parade of shops in Mackie Avenue, where an ex-BH&D Bristol Lodekka FS6B in full red and cream is about to pull up in the summer of 1971. By now the vehicle (SPM 23), dating from 1960, had gained Southdown fleetnumber 2023 but was otherwise in original condition. *Dave Brown*

First published 2004

ISBN 0 7110 3007 3

Published by Ian Allan Publishing

an imprint of Ian Allan Publishing Ltd, Hersham, Surrey KT12 4RG.
Printed by Ian Allan Printing Ltd, Hersham, Surrey KT12 4RG.

Code: 0404/B2

companies, the Bristol/Eastern Coach Works (ECW) combination soon became the standard. BH&D, however, retained much of its individuality. Protected by the 1938 agreement, it retained its livery of red with cream roof and window surrounds, as well as its non-standard destination displays. Even the earlier Lodekkas had non-standard windows with metal louvres, which gave them a very distinctive appearance.

The third company in the town was Southdown, a BET subsidiary and ardent Leyland operator, although a fair number of Guys were added to the fleet during and after World War 2. Again due to the 1938 agreement, it was necessary for Southdown to charge higher fares within the town boundaries to protect the other two operators. This state of affairs lasted until 1961, when the original agreement expired and a new one, known as the Brighton Area Transport Services (BATS) agreement was drawn up in which Southdown was included. Receipts within the area were shared between the three operators on a percentage basis in accordance with the mileage operated. The Brighton area was extended to Telscombe in the east, Shoreham in the west and Falmer and Pyecombe in the north.

Above right: In 1970 Brighton Corporation forsook its traditional colours of red and cream (shared with BH&D) in favour of blue and white, as seen freshly applied to Corporation Leyland PD2/Weymann 6 (5006 CD) labouring up St James's Street on the 42 — originally a trolleybus route — in 1973. At this time Green Shield Stamps were still very much a marketing tool, which customers could use to buy various products. It is difficult to believe today that St James's Street once handled two-way traffic. *John Bishop*

Below right: The traditional terminus for Southdown routes in Brighton was Pool Valley, which derives its name from an intermittent stream which reached the sea at this point. Following the 1961 BATS agreement this facility was 'invaded' by BH&D, which explains the presence in 1967 of the latter's Bristol Lodekka FS6B 48 (XPM 48) on local route 38, in company with Southdown Guy Arab 549 (PUF 649) on route 23 to Crawley and Leyland Leopard 116 (116 CUF) on service 180 to Heathfield and Woods Corner. *Michael Dryhurst*

The late 'Sixties and the formation of the National Bus Company saw BH&D absorbed into Southdown, whilst Brighton Corporation abandoned its familiar red and cream livery in favour of blue and white. The rear-engined bus arrived — Bristol REs and VRs and Daimler Fleetlines for Southdown/BH&D and Leyland Atlanteans and Panther Cubs for the Corporation. The latter subsequently turned to the Dennis Dominator, the Leyland National and Lynx and finally the Dennis Dart.

Privatisation of the National Bus Company saw the Brighton operations of Southdown handed over to the 'new' Brighton & Hove Bus & Coach Co — in essence a reincarnation of BH&D. After a spell as an independent operator and a resurrection of its apple-green and cream livery, Southdown was swallowed up by the Stagecoach empire in 1989. Brighton & Hove too succumbed to one of the big groups, in 1993, but the group in this case was Go-Ahead, which allowed the company to retain its livery and individuality. Such was not the case with the Corporation, by then known as Brighton Buses. When it sold out to Go-Ahead in 1997 it was, not unnaturally, merged with the Brighton & Hove fleet.

Prior to deregulation in 1986 there were few independent stage-carriage operators in Sussex, and none worked into Brighton. In fact the only other service buses to be seen in the town were the dark-green and cream ones of Maidstone & District, which operated a number of services jointly with Southdown. Over the years it used Leyland TDs, rebodied Bristols, Leyland PD2s and AEC Regent Vs before turning to 36ft AEC Reliances and Leyland Panthers. Strangely, although M&D was an early user of the type, its Atlanteans very rarely ventured as far as Brighton.

Southdown operated a wide network of express services from its cramped coach station in Steine Street, and on summer Saturdays coaches would often stretch back along Manchester Street and overflow into narrow St James's Street, then a two-way thoroughfare and trolleybus route, causing chaos as they awaited access to the coach station. Most important was the hourly service to London, operated in postwar years by ECW-bodied Leyland PS1s, all-Leyland Royal Tigers, Beadle-Commer integrals and Weymann Fanfare-bodied Leyland Tiger Cubs, before the ubiquitous Leyland Leopard took over.

Another joint operation was the South Coast Express from Margate to Bournemouth and beyond, which was operated with East Kent and Royal Blue. East Kent's immediate postwar offering was Dennis Lances followed by AEC Reliances of ever-increasing length. Royal Blue provided Bristols ranging from its elegant Duple-bodied L6Bs, through LS and MW types to the rear-engined RE.

Steine Street was home to operators from all over the country, including Black & White, Midland Red and Grey Cars, and even saw one late-evening arrival from Bradford, worked (when I remember it) by a Beadle-Commer integral of Yorkshire Woollen.

Left: The mid-1980s saw many changes to the UK bus-operating industry, notably the privatisation of the NBC and deregulation of all bus routes outside London, preparations for which included the reactivation of the dormant Brighton, Hove & District Omnibus Co. As a prelude to this, three Leyland Nationals were painted in traditional red and cream (accurate even to the original-style black fleetnumbers) to mark BH&D's 50th anniversary. No 146 (FHE 404L), recently acquired from Yorkshire Traction, is seen in August 1985 outside Whitehawk garage, still used today by Brighton & Hove Bus and Coach Co. *John Bishop*

Left: Withdean Stadium is now the temporary home of the local football team, Brighton & Hove Albion. Possibly of greater interest to transport historians is the location for the Park & Ride service into the centre of Brighton. Following seven Leyland National 2s in 1983, Brighton Buses' next new single-deckers were 12 Leyland Lynxes delivered 1988-90, one of which, 92 (G992 VWV), is seen on Park & Ride duty at the stadium car park in March 1992. *John Bishop*

Narrative by Glyn Kraemer-Johnson
Photographs selected and captioned
by John Bishop

Madeira Drive was another Mecca for the coach enthusiast, as well as being home to the British Coach Rally and the London–Brighton run of the Historic Commercial Vehicle Club (now Society), both events bringing a remarkable variety of vehicles into the town.

During the golden age of coaching in the late 'Forties and 'Fifties the western end of Madeira Drive would see, each morning, a line of excursion coaches, each with its elaborately chalked blackboard advertising its particular tour. Southdown predominated, but one would also find coaches of the three local coach operators — Campings, Alpha and Unique. Campings, with an attractive livery of turquoise and cream, began as an operator of 'heavyweights', including AEC Regals and Reliances; it also had a magnificent Commer Avenger with Harrington 'dorsal fin' body. It later changed its allegiance to Bedford and Ford and its livery to red and blue and became as much a dealer as an operator. Alpha had a pleasing black and cream livery and was a mainly Bedford operator. Unique, with a two-tone green livery, also favoured Bedfords but had the odd 'gem' such as a Harrington-bodied Leyland Comet.

To the east of the Aquarium, Madeira Drive was the province of visiting coaches, which on summer weekends, for a couple of hours in the morning, would offer a continuous procession of coaches and buses that would rival and probably outdo any modern rally. There were the regular visitors, such as Grey-Green, Orange Luxury, Banfield's, Valiant of Ealing, Timpson's, RACS and Surrey Motors, together with some less-common operators, such as Margo of Bexleyheath, Cook of Guildford, Clubb of Wilmington and a host of others, with an amazing variety of vehicles. To round off the collection there were usually some RFs, RTs, RTLs and RTWs of London Transport. The spectacle would then be repeated in reverse between 4 and 6pm.

This, then, is a brief summary of the public transport which can (or could) be seen on the streets of Brighton. In the space at our disposal we cannot hope to show more than a taste of the vast variety of types and liveries, so we apologise if your particular favourite is not included. If you like what you see, contact the publisher. We've enough material for a second volume …!

Glyn Kraemer-Johnson
Hailsham, East Sussex
January 2004

Left: Seen passing through the Old Steine on the occasion of the HCVC London–Brighton run in May 1974 is the one-time BH&D 6356 (CAP 211), a Bristol K5G with ECW bodywork, by now preserved in the livery of the Thames Valley Traction Co. Many of this batch, delivered in 1940, were rebuilt as convertible open-toppers to replace earlier ex-Tilling AEC Regents on route 17, but some remained in original condition, retaining their high radiators; upon withdrawal these were converted by BH&D as permanent open-toppers and sold for further service with Thames Valley in the Windsor area. Happily, one of the convertible versions has also been saved and is currently undergoing restoration. *Dave Brown*

Below left: For many years Brighton has been the destination of the Historic Commercial Vehicle Club (now Society) runs staged on the first Sunday in May. Enjoying a well-earned rest on Madeira Drive at the conclusion of the 1978 event is perhaps the most famous of all Brighton Corporation buses; forming part of the initial motor-bus fleet (60-80) which replaced the trams in 1939, Weymann-bodied AEC Regent No 63 (FUF 63) served the town for 26 years and has been in preservation since 1965. *Michael Dryhurst*

Right: What better way to portray 'Sussex by the Sea' than the white cliffs of the South Downs meeting the sea at Saltdean, in east Brighton. On a beautiful summer's day in the mid-1960s BH&D Bristol KS6G 496 (MPM 496) with 7ft 6in-wide ECW bodywork travels westwards towards Brighton on route 55. On the hilltop is the Ocean Hotel, and in the dip Saltdean Lido, fully restored in more recent times. The road into the background leads to Newhaven, which in this era was the preserve of Southdown Motor Services. *Howard Butler*

Left: Seen when brand-new in the summer of 1966, BH&D Bristol FLF6G/ECW 79 (HPN 79D) reaches journey's end at picturesque Rottingdean, with its quaint houses, shops and village pond. The bus exemplifies the effect achieved by the individual application of bright red and cream, complemented by black mudguards and wheels. *Howard Butler*

Above: The terminus for routes to/from Rottingdean was situated on the southern side of the crossroads on the main Brighton–Eastbourne coast road. Ex-BH&D Bristol FSF6G 32 (VAP 32), by now Southdown 2032, awaits departure on route 2 in June 1973. The informative bus stop, with distinctive white-on-black lettering, left passengers in no doubt as to the routes' respective destinations. *John Bishop*

Above: The main A259 coast road at the crossroads in Rottingdean is the setting for 994 (EHY 581), a Bristol K5G acquired by BH&D in 1955 from the Bristol Tramways Co. Dating from 1938, it had its ECW body rebuilt to open-top in BH&D's Conway Street body shop. The bus would turn to our left into a short section of road (towards the sea) that has recently been pedestrianised. *Howard Butler*

Right: In 1979 Brighton Corporation had four of its five Leyland Titan PD3s converted to open-top. They duly appeared in a variety of liveries; here 32 (LUF 132F) promotes the 'Hop on, hop off' facility available on open-top services as it prepares to leave Rottingdean for Brighton with a full load in the early 1990s. *Dave Brown*

Left: Woodingdean, in east Brighton, is on the edge of the South Downs, as is apparent from this view of Corporation Willowbrook-bodied Leyland Atlantean 88 (WUF 988K) emerging from Bexhill Road into Falmer Road in the early 1970s when still relatively new. Thankfully the South Downs is a protected area remaining unspoiled and safe from housing developers. *John Bishop*

Below left: Pictured in April 1975 *en route* to Rottingdean, Bristol Lodekka 2060 (CNJ 60B) displays a mixture of styles, the NBC lettering on traditional Southdown livery failing to disguise its BH&D origins. Delivered in 1964 as No 60, it was renumbered when absorbed into the Southdown fleet upon formation of the National Bus Company. The stretch of road between the Race Hill and Woodingdean is still open countryside today, assisted by the presence of the Racecourse located to the left of our view. *John Bishop*

Right: With the South Downs in the distance, ex-BH&D Bristol Lodekka 2082 (JPM 82D) dating from 1966 takes a breather after reaching the Race Hill via Freshfield Road. Pictured in July 1977, its full NBC livery a far cry from the superb red and cream of just a few years earlier. To add injury to insult, it would be sold the following year, as Southdown standardised on its 'Queen Mary' PD3s for the remaining ex-BH&D crew work. *John Bishop*

The Whitehawk estate in east Brighton was the terminus of routes 1 and 3. On layover in Whitehawk Avenue, overlooked by Brighton Racecourse, BH&D 462 (JAP 500) was one of a batch of 15 Bristol KSW6Gs delivered in 1954/5. Note on the nearside below the lower window the green running-plate — an example of London practice inherited from Thomas Tilling Ltd. Since this photograph was taken in the 1960s most of the original council houses have been demolished and replaced with more modern housing. *Howard Butler*

Open-top Bristol K5G/ECW 990 (GHT 125) — another vehicle acquired from Bristol Tramways and rebuilt by BH&D — drifts down past Black Rock bathing pool in the early 1960s. Visible atop the cliffs stretching away towards Rottingdean are the exclusive Roedean girls' school and, a little further on, St Dunstan's home for the blind. Likely to be of greater interest to transport historians, however, is the trackbed for the 'Daddy Longlegs' sea tram, abandoned in 1901 after only five years. In the decade after this photograph was taken the Brighton Marina would transform the area forever, and the road in the foreground would disappear. *Howard Butler*

Left: The old order and the new for Brighton Corporation in Queen's Park Road in the early Seventies. Marshall-bodied Leyland Panther Cub 42 (NUF 142G) on route 41 passes Leyland PD2/Weymann 20 (DCD 20C), converted for one-man operation; note the use of the rear destination screen to display 'PAY AS YOU ENTER'. A characteristic of buildings near to the South Downs is the use of knapped flint, as here in the case of St Luke's church. Traffic aside, the scene has changed little between the 19th century and the present day. *Malcolm Keeping*

Above: Looking from the opposite side of Queen's Park Road (and just out of view to the right of this picture) is the affectionately named 'Pepper Box', once a water/observation tower for the now demolished Italianate villa of Thomas Attree. Pausing in June 1987 is Brighton Buses Alexander-bodied Dodge minibus 59 (E459 WJK) on newly introduced 'Brighton Bustler' route 81, which replaced the familiar 42. Despite the loss of its trams, Brighton retained some remnants of its once-proud system, notably some ornate wooden tram shelters, one of which can be seen on the right. *John Bishop*

Left: Having climbed Elm Grove (see back cover), circular routes 41 and 42 would turn right and make their way south back towards the town centre. Pictured early in 1964, Corporation AEC Regent/Weymann 61 (FUF 61) of 1939 prepares to overtake a parked three-wheeler in Queen's Park Road. The trolleybus poles were still evident at this time, even though half a decade had passed since the trolleybuses' withdrawal. *John Bishop*

Above: Mention the words 'global warming' in the early 1960s and no one would have known the meaning of the expression. On a grim winter's day

Southdown all-Leyland Titan PD2 348 (JCD 48) on route 42 emerges from Queen's Park Road into Elm Grove before descending towards Lewes Road. Southdown operated the occasional journey on service 42 to balance mileage under the terms of the BATS agreement. These were the days when 20 Cadets cigarettes cost 2s 10d (14p) or 3s 5d (17½p), depending upon whether they were plain or filter-tipped. Today Elm Grove is lined with cars belonging to residents or visitors to Brighton General Hospital, visible in the distance. *Malcolm Keeping*

A spring view, recorded in the early Seventies, opposite St Joseph's church at the bottom of Elm Grove, up which buses would labour fully laden on race days. A decade had now passed since trolleybuses would tackle the steep gradient as if it were flat terrain. Ex-BH&D Bristol KS6G 496 (MPM 496), by now 2496 in the Southdown fleet, is evasive as to its destination; in those days there was no such display as 'Sorry — not in service'! This was one of the last Bristol Ks built, in 1957, by which time most of Bristol's double-deck production had switched to the Lodekka; Brighton, however, had no need of a low-height capability but required narrow buses for negotiating the congested St James's Street (then a two-way thoroughfare!) on route 3. Elm Grove is still instantly recognisable today, having been spared by the developers.
Dave Brown

Heading south along the Lewes Road towards the Old Steine in September 1977 is Corporation 21 (21 ACD), a Leyland PD2 and one of the early PAYE conversions. In progress in the background are the final stages of the dismantling of the railway viaduct which carried the Kemp Town branch — long closed to passengers but retained until the early 1970s for goods traffic.

Unwittingly the photographer has also captured what was probably a low-point in the life of the Volkswagen Beetle owner, who is being apprehended by the Sussex Police Traffic Officer! Both the VW and the police Ford Granada would now be regarded as classics in their own right. *Dave Brown*

Left: Captured in Lewes Road opposite its garage is Corporation Leyland PD2/Metro-Cammell 51 (WCD 51), still in the red and cream livery — albeit with a blue offside front wheel! Sadly neither of the department stores advertised survives today; Hanningtons — 'Brighton's Leading Department Store' — closed as recently as 2001, vacating a prominent city-centre site yet to be filled, while Johnson Bros suffered a disastrous fire in 1970 from which it never fully recovered, despite subsequently trading from alternative premises. Following withdrawal from passenger service, 51 served as a driver trainer before joining the ranks of preserved ex-Brighton Corporation buses, although regrettably it has since fallen into disrepair. *John Bishop*

Left: By May 1973 days were numbered for Corporation Leyland Titan PD2 No 58 (WCD 58), its Metro-Cammell Orion bodywork largely devoid of advertisements. The buildings on the far left formed part of Preston Barracks, built originally in 1795, when this locale fell within the (then) separate parish of Preston. Much of the site has now been redeveloped as a retail park, although a reduced area has been retained for use by the Territorial Army. The large block in the far distance is the Cockroft Building, part of Brighton Polytechnic (nowadays Brighton University). *John Bishop*

The front of Brighton Corporation's offices and garage, on the opposite side of the Lewes Road, was always impressive, as is apparent from this view of dual-door East Lancs-bodied Leyland Atlantean 72 (OYJ 72R) in August 1977 when still quite new. Introduced in 1970, the Corporation's new livery of blue and white had initially retained the same layout as the red and cream used previously but from 1974 was brightened by reversing the colours of the upper deck, giving greater prominence to the white, here being used to its full advantage for advertising. The tall building immediately to the left of the bus is the Allen West factory, where much of the electrical equipment for Brighton's trolleybuses was produced and which is now a storage centre. Lewes Road garage remains in use today with Brighton & Hove Bus and Coach Co.
Dave Brown

Between the Lewes Road and Ditchling Road is the large housing estate at Hollingdean, with its pleasant mix of private and council housing, first developed in the 1890s but not completed until the 1960s. The latter decade also witnessed the birth of the allover-advertisement bus, to boost operators' revenue and maximise publicity for the client. Some liveries were hideous, to say the least, whilst others, including that on Brighton Corporation 2 (TYJ 2S), promoting Phoenix Assurance, were striking yet pleasing to the eye. An East Lancs-bodied Leyland Atlantean new in 1978, the bus is seen leaving Hollingdean in June 1982. *John Bishop*

Under the terms of the BATS agreement Brighton Corporation was responsible for providing bus services to Hollingdean. In 1983 these were recast with the advent of the popular high-frequency 'Shuttle' service 50, as part of a joint innovation with Southdown, which operated the Mile Oak Shuttle (60).

In dedicated Hollingdean Shuttle livery, Brighton Leyland National 2 No 29 (XFG 29Y) waits to emerge into Hollingdean Road *en route* to the town centre via Ditchling Road in August 1983. *John Bishop*

Above: The Dennis Dominator enjoyed a brief popularity in the late 1970s and early '80s, Brighton Corporation changing allegiance to order a pair with East Lancs bodywork for delivery in 1981. No 17 (OAP 17W) is seen in May 1982 in the large housing estate at Bevendean, off the main Lewes Road out of Brighton. Even 20 years ago the number of parked cars was still acceptable, but the scene is very different today. *John Bishop*

Right: In 1980 Brighton Corporation took advantage of London Transport's sale of its DMS class of Daimler Fleetlines, acquiring two and numbering them 91/2. Resplendent in blue and white, No 92 (MLK 558L) was photographed in September 1981 at the Bevendean terminus of route 11, which ran across Brighton to another postwar housing estate, at Hangleton, Hove. *John Bishop*

Above: On the A27 trunk road to Lewes, the village of Falmer nowadays marks the boundary between Brighton & Hove and East Sussex. Our late-1960s view shows the then main road, with the 'Swan' public house to our left and Campings Coaches' Plaxton-bodied Ford R226 EMJ 357E speeding past towards Brighton on a cold and frosty day. One of Brighton's three independent coach companies (the others being Alpha and Unique), Campings would be acquired by Brighton Borough Transport on 1 July 1989. This section of road is now by-passed by the dual carriageway driven through the village in the 1970s, changing the whole appearance of the area and leaving residents to the constant roar of speeding cars and lorries. *Michael Dryhurst*

Right: West of the A27 Lewes Road is the estate of Coldean, served by Southdown route 13 under the terms of the BATS agreement. In this stunning early-1960s view 1948 all-Leyland Titan PD2 326 (JCD 26) approaches Old Boat Corner (where an upturned boat had once served as a shepherd's hut) on its way to Coldean. The area here has undergone dramatic change, with the A27 Brighton by-pass slicing through the South Downs to connect with the A23 London Road and onwards to Shoreham. Just savour this tranquil scene! *Howard Butler*

Before the BATS agreement between the three main operators it would have been unheard of to see a Southdown bus on the 15 route, which operated between Patcham, in north Brighton, and Upper Portslade. No 351 (JCD 51), an all-Leyland PD2 of 1948, heads up Ladies Mile Road, Patcham, displaying a black-on-white blind of the 'lazy' variety, which did not need changing at termini. Such blinds were but temporary and a rare sight on a Southdown bus. The location is little changed today save for the inevitable presence of the motor car. *Howard Butler*

In the 1960s Ladies Mile Road was still on the edge of open downland, as
apparent from this view looking north towards Ditchling Beacon. Delivered in
1951, BH&D 426 (FNJ 108) was a Bristol KS5G with an 8ft-wide ECW body
on its 7ft 6in chassis, the inset wheels emphasising its narrow track.
Howard Butler

Patcham was served by BH&D's 5 group of routes as well as by the 15. The terminus of the 5 was (and is) the parade of shops in Mackie Avenue, seen on a cold January day in 1964 — a time when winters seem to have been harsher than they are today. As BH&D Bristol KSW6G 452 (HAP 990) waits time at the terminus, a similar bus in the background has given up and will reverse to fill the space vacated in due course by 452. *Howard Butler*

Braeside Avenue, Patcham, looks idyllic with manicured grass verges, semi-detached houses and bungalows; throw in BH&D Bristol K6B/ECW 384 (CPN 9) and your author is in Heaven! Delivered in 1947, these vehicles represented an end to wartime restrictions on build quality and served Brighton faithfully for over 15 years, this example being seen *c*1963 in its last days of service. *Howard Butler*

Above: On the western side of the London Road is the post war estate of Westdene, which adjoins the older-established Withdean. This view at Withdean Stadium gives some idea how steep and tortuous the roads around Brighton can be, especially for a double-deck bus; Brighton Buses 72 (OYJ 72R), a dual-door East Lancs-bodied Leyland Atlantean new in 1977, stands at the leafy terminus of route 10 in March 1992. *John Bishop*

Right: A quite remarkable picture, taken in the 1960s, portraying road and rail travel. Stealing the show, with safety valve blowing off, is none other than Gresley Pacific No 4472 *Flying Scotsman*, visiting Brighton on an excursion. Meanwhile, being pursued north along the main A23 London Road by a little Ford Prefect is a Harrington-bodied Bedford SB in the distinctive two-tone green of Unique Coaches. Although this operator no longer trades, its depot (near Brighton station) remains in use. Sadly this location is unrecognisable today, as most (if not all) of the houses have been demolished to make way for flats. *Howard Butler*

Left: Preston Circus was the junction of the A23 London Road and A27 Lewes–Brighton–Hove road until the Brighton by-pass was built. When this photograph was taken in the early 1960s there really was a roundabout (just visible on the left), but this has since been removed in the interest of 'traffic management' (although the junction still sees tremendous jams, especially at peak times). BH&D Bristol KSW6G 445 (GPN 993) is bound for the Seven Dials terminus of route 44, which until March 1959 had been the preserve of BH&D trolleybuses. The building behind is the town's main fire station and bears traces of Brighton's trolleybuses in the form of eyelets for the span wire. *Howard Butler*

Above: To the south and east of Patcham is Hollingbury, a large housing estate developed postwar close to the site of an Iron Age hill fort. Demonstrating the value of the tilt test, BH&D Bristol KSW6G/ECW 472 (JAP 510) dating from 1955 leans alarmingly as it turns into Carden Hill. The lack of other traffic and parked cars is very noticeable in this 1960s view. Note also the lady passenger judging her moment to bail out! *Howard Butler*

Above: Brighton Corporation's trolleybuses reached Hollingbury only in 1951, yet in 10 years the whole system would be abandoned. Seen *c*1959, Weymann-bodied AEC trolleybus 20 (FUF 20) of 1939 still looks pristine in the bright sunshine. Whilst some development has taken place the South Downs conservationists have thankfully ensured this area has changed little since this photograph was taken. *Marcus Eavis*

Right: For many, Hollingbury will always be associated with the northern extremities of the trolleybus system (routes 26 and 46), partly because the scene has remained much the same for the last 40 years. This view looks in the opposite direction to that in the previous picture. Seen shortly before withdrawal, in May 1973, BH&D Lodekka 45 (XPM 45) has been renumbered 2045 in the Southdown fleet but retains full red-and-cream livery. *John Bishop*

Left: The trolleybuses proved their effectiveness on route 26, showing a good turn of speed on the climb from Hollingbury to Ditchling Road. Bound for the Old Steine in 1961, Corporation 41 (FUF 41), a Weymann-bodied AEC, romps up Carden Hill through the huge postwar council estate. Note the red tarmacadam then popular in Brighton.
E. C. Bennett & Martin Jenkins/ Online Transport Archive

Right: From the previous view we have now reached the top of Carden Hill and joined Ditchling Road for the long descent to the centre of Brighton. In the spring of 1961 No 1 (FUF 1) has just passed (right) the site of the aforementioned hill fort. The old tram shelter was repositioned from another site in the town (the trams never having operated this far out of Brighton), while the large layby served as the trolleybuses' original turning circle, before the route was extended to Hollingbury; both survive to this day as reminders of earlier modes of transport in Brighton.
E. C. Bennett & Martin Jenkins/ Online Transport Archive

Right: In the spring of 1961, with the flowering cherry in full bloom, Corporation AEC/Weymann trolleybus 17 (FUF 17) descends the steep, lower section of Ditchling Road on its way to the Old Steine on route 26A. Increased road traffic (and parking) aside, this is another scene which has changed little during the intervening 43 years.
E. C. Bennett & Martin Jenkins/ Online Transport Archive

Left: Having reached the bottom of Ditchling Road, we travel by trolleybus along Union Road to the Lewes Road at Richmond Terrace, where this picture of BH&D 346 (CPM 521) on circular route 41 was taken in 1959. In the pooling agreement with Brighton Corporation BH&D operated 11 trolleybuses, of which eight (including 346) were Weymann-bodied AECs. All BH&D's AEC trolleybuses were withdrawn and scrapped except for 342 (CPM 61), which was secured for preservation after the first stage of abandonment in 1959. Behind the photographer is The Level, a large area of open land undeveloped in the 19th century on account of its then swampy nature and today used primarily as a fairground. *A. P. Tatt Transport Collection*

Left: We have now reached St Peter's church (to our right), site of the junction between the A23 London Road and the A27 Lewes Road. Present on a murky day in the late Fifties are an almost brand-new KS6G of BH&D and a Corporation AEC trolleybus. The former is 499 (MPM 499), numerically the penultimate Bristol K to be built, in 1957. Distinctive features are the full fleetname and full destination blind; however, it is interesting to note that, despite the use of a full destination blind, route boards were often inserted and the clips are visible below the destination screen fitted from new. Route 14 would later be renumbered 54 to avoid confusion with Southdown's 14. *A. P. Tatt Transport Collection*

Long gone are the days when the streets of Brighton thronged with trolleybuses making their way to the Old Steine! Having descended Elm Grove from the Race Hill on route 43A, Corporation AEC/Weymann 34 (FUF 34), pictured opposite St Peter's church (left), is on the last leg of its journey, with the first (and last) trolleybus, No 1, following in hot pursuit. Despite the absence of some of the large trees, destroyed in the infamous hurricane of 1987, the area remains instantly recognisable today. *Marcus Eavis*

Heading north towards Hollingbury, Corporation AEC/Weymann trolleybus 24 (FUF 24) of 1939 has left London Road and is approaching St Peter's church (to our right). Whilst this is another scene still easily recognisable, the buildings behind have been rebuilt; thankfully, however, this was no repeat of the indiscriminate demolition of earlier years, as the frontages have been retained, preserving the character of the area. *A. P. Tatt Transport Collection*

Brighton's parish church, St Peter's was built in the 1820s and is now a listed building, although its future in its present form is currently in doubt, on account of the extraordinary sums needed to repair and maintain it. The hurricane of 1987 decimated the majestic trees seen here in the spring of 1961, with Corporation AEC/Weymann trolleybus 23 (FUF 23) bound for the Old Steine on route 26. Behind is an unidentified Corporation AEC Regent III, while in the distance another trolleybus is emerging into the Richmond Terrace from St Peter's Place. Impeding No 23 is locally registered Dennis lorry; just visible on the left is a Morris J van of the Initial laundry, ahead of which is a Lambretta scooter with helmet-less rider — a reminder of a more relaxed era. *E. C. Bennett & Martin Jenkins/ Online Transport Archive*

46

Left: Rear views are often neglected, especially in the case of a bus with an exposed radiator. In this June 1971 picture, Corporation Leyland PD3/MCW 31 (LUF 131F) and Southdown Bristol VR/ECW 508 (TCD 508J) are seen just to the north of the famous Royal Pavilion, in Marlborough Place. The distinctive Tudor-fronted building is the King & Queen public house, actually built as recently as the 1930s to replace a much earlier structure which was originally a farmhouse. The right-hand side of the road is now a permanent bus lane, to keep the buses moving through the ever-increasing traffic congestion suffered in this part of central Brighton. *Dave Brown*

Above: A sight to make any Leyland enthusiast weep! Corporation Leyland PD2/ Weymann 19 (DCD 19C), immaculate in newly applied French blue and white, receives the attentions of the fleet's AEC Matador breakdown lorry at the Old Steine in 1971. No fleetname is carried, as the sloping '*BRIGHTON CORPORATION*' style was about to be adopted. Note also the 'PAY AS YOU ENTER' notice by the entrance — unusual on a half-cab type and a reminder that the Corporation had converted such buses to PAYE operation in the 1960s. *Dave Brown*

Left: By May 1971 much of the Brighton Corporation fleet had already been repainted from its familiar red and cream to blue and white, as demonstrated by the three Corporation vehicles in this view in the Old Steine. Marshall-bodied Leyland Panther Cub 39 (NUF 139G) of 1968 is about to be passed by Weymann-bodied Leyland PD2 19 (DCD 19C) dating from 1965, both on routes now long gone. The buildings beyond the second PD2, Nos 3 and 4 Old Steine, date from 1790 and are the survivors of four known as the 'Blues & Buffs', having originally been painted in the colours of the Whig party to please the then Prince of Wales (later George IV). *Dave Brown*

Above: Almost the exact-same location a couple of years earlier, in May 1969. Strachans-bodied Leyland Panther Cub 38 (NUF 138G) looks resplendent in its original livery of red and cream, complete with Brighton County Borough coat of arms, as it passes the bottom of St James's Street, but regrettably these handsome buses would have woefully short lives, on account of their unreliability. Note the array of British cars, especially the green Austin A35 (right) with its new reflective numberplates and bright wheeltrims. The ground floor of St James's Mansions, then a BR travel office, now houses Brighton & Hove Bus and Coach Co's 'One Stop Travel' shop. *Dave Brown*

Left: Firm favourites with both authors were the handsome Weymann-bodied AEC Regent IIIs, delivered in two batches in 1947 and 1950. No 88 (HUF 88) of 1947 is seen in the early 1960s emerging from St James's Street into the Old Steine — a manœuvre impossible nowadays, the road being one-way. Note the artistic lettering for J. Lyons, later simplified in order to update the image; also the early 'No Waiting' sign, next to which a chivalrous gentleman is coaxing fellow pedestrians across the icy road. *Howard Butler*

Above: St James's Street could be termed 'the gateway to Kemp Town' and boasted many shops, including the Green Shield Stamp outlet visible immediately behind Bristol RESL/ECW 2202 (PPM 202G) in this 1973 photograph. New to BH&D in 1968, the bus was by now part of the Southdown fleet and would soon be repainted leaf green. At this time two-way traffic was permitted, but today vehicles may travel only in an easterly direction. *John Bishop*

Right: In the early part of the 20th century the Old Steine was the hub of the Brighton Corporation Tramways network, with routes radiating to all corners of the town. The shortest of these was route S to Brighton station, represented by Class F car 52. In this view — the first of three recorded during the spring of 1939 — the trees are in full foliage, whilst the pedestrians display the fashions for flowing wide trousers and greased hair and are mostly hat-wearers. The car itself, with simplified livery and smaller fleetname, had been built as recently as 1937 but would nevertheless be withdrawn within a couple of months of this photograph being taken. *Leeds Transport Historical Society, courtesy Online Transport Archive*

Left: Displaying an earlier, more decorative style of livery, Class E tram No 77, built in 1931, stands in front of the ornate wooden shelter-cum-office which would survive well into the 1970s before being replaced by an anonymous-looking structure. The tram itself was scrapped later in 1939 following the cessation of tramway operation, route D, involving a steep climb up Ditchling Road (see page 40) from the centre of Brighton, being replaced by trolleybus routes 26 and 26A on 1 June. *Leeds Transport Historical Society, courtesy Online Transport Archive*

Right: The end is nigh! With a tram standing defiantly behind, new AEC/Weymann trolleybus 3 (FUF 3) gleams in the sunshine as it sets off for Preston Barracks in Lewes Road on route 48. Note the chrome front hubcaps, which would not last long before the red paintbrush was applied. Tram route L, which the 48 replaced, was the first to succumb, on 1 May 1939, but ironically the track had to be left in place to permit access to the Lewes Road depot for the remainder of the tram fleet, until their final demise on 31 August 1939. *Leeds Transport Historical Society, courtesy Online Transport Archive*

Left: The Old Steine remained the hub of Brighton Corporation's routes, although (as in tram days) the destination was always displayed as 'Aquarium'. In the summer of 1959 — some 20 years after the trams' withdrawal — AEC trolleybuses 31 and 20 on Hollingbury routes 26 and 46 jostle for position with a pair of AEC Regents; note the similarity of the Weymann bodywork. *Marcus Eavis*

Above: In 1961 a fire at Weymann's delayed the delivery of Brighton's new Leyland PD2s, and as a stopgap to replace the trolleybuses it was necessary for the Corporation to purchase second-hand from Southdown four prewar Leyland Titan TD5s, including 20 (FCD 510). All had been rebodied postwar, in this case by East Lancs — a builder which would come to figure largely in Corporation orders. In this view at the Old Steine the trolleybuses have gone and the wiring has been dismantled. The trolleybus poles supporting the lights had a definite lean without the tension of the wires! Like the TD5s, these were short-lived, as new lights were soon installed. *John Bishop*

ST. HELENS ESTATE

5 B

HAP
996

Left: ECW-bodied Bristol KSW6G 2458 (HAP 996) speeds through the Old Steine on route 5B to St Helen's Estate in Hangleton, Hove, in June 1971. This, apparently, was a time when children wore shawls regardless of how hot it was! *Dave Brown*

Above: With the Old Steine in the background, BH&D Bristol RESL 210 (PPM 210G) negotiates the Aquarium roundabout as it turns onto the seafront in November 1968. The 10 buses of this batch were the first saloons for nearly 30 years but, with their handsome ECW bodywork and attractive livery style, were well in keeping with BH&D tradition. Like the rest of the batch, this bus passed to Southdown (as 2210), with which it saw out its service in Portsmouth, before being sold to an independent operator in Somerset. Happily it was later restored to BH&D livery and is now in the hands of local enthusiasts. *Michael Dryhurst*

Above: Having arrived from Hawkhurst, Maidstone & District S53 (EKJ 113C), a Weymann-bodied AEC Reliance of 1965, stands in Pool Valley bus station when still quite new. Pool Valley would undergo renovation in the 1990s, at which time the old Southdown lettering on the booking office (visible here behind S53 but later hidden behind a new fascia) was revealed. Today most 'country' buses terminate at Churchill Square, Pool Valley being used principally by National Express coaches. *Malcolm Keeping*

Right: Seen in the Old Steine outside Royal York Buildings, two of Southdown's 'Queen Mary' Northern Counties-bodied Leyland PD3s, on route 13 to Coldean, obscure the awkward entrance to Pool Valley bus station. No 422 (422 DCD) has a convertible-open-top body, while 367 (HCD 367E) was one of the final batch, with panoramic windows. The Royal Albion Hotel (far left) would suffer severe fire damage in 1998 but fortunately was rebuilt and still stands proudly on the corner of Grand Junction Road opposite the Palace Pier (nowadays known simply as 'Brighton Pier') and the Aquarium (now the 'Sea Life Centre'). *John Bishop*

Above: A superb picture taken in Castle Square, at the bottom of North Street; as its name suggests, Pavilion Buildings (right) leads to the Royal Pavilion. (The 'castle' was the Castle Inn, demolished in the early 19th century.) Corporation Leyland PD2/Weymann 15 (5015 CD) was delivered in 1961 to complete the replacement of Brighton's trolleybuses and was already 10 years old when this view was recorded in June 1971. Streamline taxis, in the familiar colours of black with cream bonnet, were then a familiar sight on the streets of Brighton and Hove, while Lloyds' Bank's merger with the TSB was still a quarter-century off. *Dave Brown*

Right: It is 10.18am by the clock of the Alliance Building Society on a warm and sunny spring day in North Street in May 1971 — the third year since 'big brother' Southdown took over BH&D. Southdown (ex-BH&D) Bristol FSF6B 2040 (WNJ 40) is on route 26 from Hollingbury to Mile Oak. The 39, however, was still operated by Brighton Corporation, as demonstrated by 34 (MCD 134F), a Metro-Cammell-bodied Leyland Titan PD3 still in red and cream and with 'PAY AS YOU ENTER' notice on the bulkhead. On the left, Hannington's department store is still 30 years from closing. *Dave Brown*

Above: A picture taken on a very hot day in the summer of 1959 in North Street, outside Alliance House, HQ of the then Alliance Building Society (and now upmarket flats). In the circumstances it is somewhat surprising to see BH&D 357 (CAP 212), a Bristol K5G with convertible BH&D body, with its roof on. At this time the bus shelters were of concrete construction, but these would give way to more modern types suitable for advertisements, to increase revenues. *Ian Stewart*

Right: Brand-new buses always look good, especially in brilliant sunshine, as here in the summer of 1959. Corporation Leyland PD2/Metro-Cammell 74 (WCD 74) picks up passengers in North Street on route 7B to the village of Ovingdean, within the Brighton boundary. Brighton Corporation was well known for its advertisements, but 74 is so new that it has not yet gained these on either side of its destination box. Brickwoods Brewery, whose product is promoted on the offside, was still independent. The splendid brick-built church in the background is the Chapel Royal, built 1793-5 to attract the Prince Regent but substantially remodelled in its present Renaissance style in the period 1876-82. *Ian Stewart*

Left: In the early 1980s Brighton Corporation introduced a further livery revision with greater areas of blue, and in the authors' opinion this represented an improvement. East Lancs-bodied Leyland Atlantean 71 (OYJ 71R) stands alongside Willowbrook-bodied 85 (TUF 85J) at Brighton station in May 1982. *John Bishop*

Above: Time was when Southdown buses on route 12 to Eastbourne would depart from the forecourt of Brighton station. The practice was revived in 1983, when Brighton Borough Transport introduced 'Shuttle' route 99 from the station to Churchill Square — a distance of half a mile. The route proved popular, and added interest was provided by the vehicles used — three of only four Bedford JJLs built, bodied by Marshall. No 36 (UKK 335X) prepares to leave the station forecourt in August 1988. Today buses no longer use the forecourt of Brighton station. *John Bishop*

The scene outside Brighton station in the early 1960s. The trolleybus poles are still standing, but the trolleys themselves have been gone five years or so. Awaiting passengers for circular route 42, once worked by trolleybuses, is not the usual Corporation bus but Southdown Park Royal-bodied Leyland Titan PD2/12 766 (OCD 766), complete with full destination display. Such odd workings arose from the need to balance mileages in order to honour the terms of the BATS agreement — much to the delight of enthusiasts! This location is much the same today but, alas, minus the red Morris J Post Office van and, of course, the PD2! *Howard Butler*

Ex-London Transport 1946 Bristol K6A No 998 (HGC 244), with ECW body dating from 1955, heads down Dyke Road, Brighton (on the boundary with Hove), towards Seven Dials. By the early 1960s most BH&D vehicles had 'T'-type blind layout displaying just route number and ultimate destination, but 998 retained its full display until withdrawal in 1964. On the right of the picture is one of the hand carts then still used by tradesmen. *Howard Butler*

Left: Returning to North Street, we look west from the Clock Tower towards Western Road, with individual small shops, as it was before Churchill Square was built. BH&D Bristol K5G/ECW 414 (EPM 11) heads for Patcham on route 5, passing the recently (2003) demolished Quadrant on the right. The 1930s building behind embodies the Imperial Arcade, once regarded as the last word in shopping but alas now a mere shadow of its former glory. *Howard Butler*

Above: An early-1970s view of the junction of Western Road and North Street, showing just how much has changed. The roof of the Regent ballroom in the centre skyline is long gone, forsaken for Boots, while Dunn & Co shops, once such a feature of our main streets, are now but a memory. Also consigned to history are Bristol Lodekka 2081 (JPM 81D), still in BH&D red and cream, and, travelling in the opposite direction, dual-door Bristol VR 528 (WUF 528K), recently delivered in green and cream with 'SOUTHDOWN-BH&D' fleetnames. *John Bishop*

Left: Western Road is Brighton main east–west shopping thoroughfare and extends into Hove. This picture, taken from the top deck of another bus of approaching BH&D Bristol KSW6G/ECW 2464 (JAP 502) on route 43 to the Race Hill, shows the view westwards *c*1970. In the background are two Corporation Leyland Titans with Metro-Cammell Orion bodies, on their regular haunt on route 49. *Dave Brown*

Above: Another view of busy Western Road, this time in the early 1960s, showing the nearside rear of BH&D 384 (CPN 9), an ECW-bodied Bristol K6B of 1947. This combination was the standard BH&D bus after the war and remained thus until the first Lodekkas arrived in 1959. Even the advertisement on the rear is a classic; Brickwoods Ales had purchased Portsmouth United Ales, which had a number of pubs in Brighton, but was itself ultimately taken over by Whitbread. *Howard Butler*

The ex-London Transport B-class Bristol K6As (with AEC engines) came to BH&D in 1953 with Duple utility bodies but were soon rebodied by ECW, in which form they operated until 1964, mostly (as here) on route 3. No 999 (HGC 254) was originally numbered 5999; under 'Tilling' numbering all second-hand vehicles were given a '5' prefix rather than '6'. Note the period chemist and, on the far left, the Curzon Cinema, where your author watched many a film! *Howard Butler*

Right: In recent years Western Road has 'benefited' from various traffic-calming measures, including narrowing of the road, the introduction of speed humps (now removed) and the restriction of traffic to buses and taxis. None of these measures was in place — or, indeed, necessary — when BH&D 457 (HAP 995) was photographed in splendid isolation in August 1966. The bus is an ECW-bodied Bristol KSW6G with number/destination display modified to match the 'T' layout of Bristol Lodekkas then being delivered. British Home Stores would move to the new Churchill Square complex when this opened in 1967. *Howard Butler*

Below right: It is the summer of 1966, and *Mary Poppins* is showing at the Curzon Cinema, in Western Road, Brighton, near the boundary with Hove — nowadays part of the joint city of Brighton & Hove but then fiercely proud of its independence. The Curzon later became the Classic (see page 70) but has now been absorbed by the Waitrose supermarket outside which rare Bristol FSF6G 35 (VAP 35), with forward-entrance ECW body, has stopped to collect passengers on its way to Rottingdean. Note the pre-decimal prices of the sewing machines in the Singer shop! *Howard Butler*

Above: No book illustrating the streets of Brighton would be complete without a photograph of the seafront. Bound for Hove on route 52, Weymann-bodied Corporation AEC Regent III 92 (KCD 92) heads along King's Road in the early 1960s. The Old Ship Hotel and Queen's Hotel survive, and the lights are still maintained in their Edwardian style, but the bus, alas, has long since passed into history. Although recorded in the early 1960s, the scene is surprisingly tranquil compared with today, when cars battle for spaces in the city-centre car parks. *Howard Butler*

Right: Until NBC days the seafront represented Southdown's only means of escape westwards! In the mid-1960s all-Leyland PD2/12 742 (LUF 242) passes Regency Square on the long run to Midhurst on route 22; out of view over the photographer's right shoulder is the ill-fated West Pier. On the left is Brighton's memorial to the men of the Royal Sussex Regiment who fell in the Boer War, while just discernible to the right of the bus is the KingsWest nightclub/cinema complex, built in the 1960s to a design intended for Montreal but considered by many to be out of place amid the mainly Regency buildings on Brighton's seafront. *Howard Butler*

Notwithstanding the delivery of new Lodekkas, for much of the 1960s the mainstay of the BH&D fleet was the Bristol KSW6G with 8ft-wide ECW bodywork — a type which would serve the residents of Brighton and Hove into the early 1970s. One of the later deliveries, 488 (LNJ 488) was nevertheless already 10 years old when this view was recorded in August 1966 at Hove station. The white-painted building visible on the left is the original station, incorporated into a new structure (just off camera) in 1879.
Howard Butler

Church Road is the main thoroughfare through Hove, being the continuation of Western Road. Still on its old 5B haunt in the early Seventies, repainted ex-BH&D Bristol FLF6G 2073 (FPM 73C) prepares to turn right into Tisbury Road; Hove Town Hall is just out of view to the left. Looking smart in Southdown green and cream with gold 'SOUTHDOWN-BH&D' fleetnames, the bus nevertheless did not seem 'right' to those used to years of red-and-cream buses. The location is much the same today. *John Bishop*

Left: We may be critical of our roads today, but just look at the surface of Kingsway in this 1960s view of Hove seafront near Hove Lagoon! The road to the right leads to Aldrington Basin and Shoreham Harbour, the junction being nowadays controlled by traffic lights and fortunately in a very much better condition than that seen here. The bus is BH&D Bristol KSW6B 433 (GNJ 998) dating from 1952, with comprehensive destination display for route 8. *Howard Butler*

Below left: During World War 2 BH&D received 12 buses to utility specification — two Guy Arabs and 10 Bristol K6As. The Guys were sold in the late 1940s to Western National, but the Bristols were subjected to thorough rebuilds, many losing their AEC engines in favour of Gardner 5LWs. No 6374 (CPM 16), rebodied by ECW, is seen in Station Road, Portslade, on a murky day in *c*1960. Nowadays part of the city of Brighton & Hove (and the borough of Hove before that), Portslade was once a separate township; the erstwhile boundary runs down the centre of the road, the other side being known as Boundary Road, Hove! *Michael Dryhurst*

Above: In the mid-1970s the most westerly destination for Brighton Corporation buses was the Southwick Green terminus of service 49, in West Sussex. Seen waiting to begin the long journey to East Moulsecoomb in Brighton on a cold day in January 1975, 15 (5015 CD), a Weymann-bodied Leyland PD2/37, seems a little shy as to its ownership, lacking a fleetname on the offside but displaying the Brighton coat of arms on the front. *John Bishop*

Above: The front of Brighton station in 1938. 'F'-class tram No 49, built in the Brighton Corporation depot at Lewes Road in 1936, prepares to leave for the Aquarium via North Road on route S (for 'Station'). Despite being only two years old, it would meet its end just a year later, in 1939, when all the trams gave way to a new fleet of trolleybuses and motor buses. On the station forecourt, preparing to depart for Eastbourne on service 12, is a Southdown '1400'-class Leyland Tiger single-decker with Harrington bus bodywork in the prewar livery incorporating a cream roof. Streamline taxis, with their smart black paintwork and cream bonnets, were long a feature of the streets of Brighton. *from a painting by Glyn Kraemer-Johnson*

Back cover: Brighton is surrounded by steep hills, including the gruelling Elm Grove, which links the Lewes Road with the Race Hill. Giving some idea is this view, recorded in June 1974, of Brighton Corporation 14 (5014 CD), a Leyland PD2 with forward-entrance Weymann bodywork. In hot pursuit is Southdown 541 (WUF 541K), a dual-door ECW-bodied Bristol VR, on erstwhile trolleybus route 44; this was one of a number of locations where Brighton's trolleybuses could use their superior power and acceleration to good advantage. *Dave Brown*